Over Morning Coffee

Jessica G Rivera - Perez

BookLeaf Publishing

Presentation by *BookLeaf Publishing*

Web: www.bookleafpub.com

E-mail: info@bookleafpub.com

ISBN: 978-93-95950-01-5

First edition 2022

.

DEDICATION

Milo, Mimi & Rory: this is for you.

ACKNOWLEDGEMENT

I would like to thank my husband, Rodolfo Perez, for always supporting me in everything I have ever faced and my family for all of their love and encouragement throughout my life.

PREFACE

I write to know myself. To understand myself. As much as therapy and speaking of things one doesn't want to speak of with a stranger helps, it helps me to write things down. This collection came together by itself. I sit, thinking every morning and over my cup of coffee, words just flow together and seem to spill over just like the cold foam I add. A lot of the times I have felt unable to speak, unable to piece together my thoughts and restrained. Many times in life we are forced into silence, forced to keep quiet and forced to hide feelings, thoughts and expressions. But we shouldn't. We should feel comfortable enough and open enough to speak of our experiences. Our lives. Our ways. We are all unique. We are all important.

Infinite

If I have fallen,
I have been picked up
If I have failed
I have also succeeded.
Everything goes both ways
Nothing is permanent
Nothing is forever
Live your life the way you want
Find your happiness
It is all that matters

BFF

What is a best friend?
Someone I can count on
A support
Someone I know will be there
The only person who keeps my secrets
Who knows me and loves me
Who sees beyond my words
Looks into my eyes and sees the unspoken
Who always has words of encouragement
Who never falters or wavers

Grief

It still hurts. If I think and ponder on it long enough it feels like a scab I am picking at. Just under the surface the skin is still raw and bleeds. It hasn't healed. I haven't healed. The truth is I'm afraid to. I'm afraid of not feeling this rawness. If I don't feel this pain, if I don't carry it with me what does that mean? I want to hold on. I don't want to say good-bye. I don't want to forget. So to this feeling I cling, until my heart atrophies.

Whistler

As long as we were together everything would work out. Everything would stay the same. We would smile without thinking anything would change. We laughed at the many impressions you made. We listened as you told the stories of when you were growing up. You were always the life of the party. You made everything fun. You taught us so much about the world around us, every talk turning into a lesson. We didn't know how good we had it. I would trade anything in the world for a do over. Anything I have or will ever have. I would give it all up if it meant you were here. If it meant you were around.

Church

Somehow, some way I am blessed
I didn't need to be
I don't deserve it
I am imperfect
But it remains
I live a good life
I have a wonderful husband
I have amazing kids
I believe in God's blessings
I have faith.

Denny's

Nausea and fatigue
The beginning
The end of the race to the center
The secret of the universe

Fast forward ten months
Ten fingers, ten toes
Beautiful brown eyes and soft pink cheeks
To think it started with two pink lines

Core

We go through many emotions
Happiness at times
And try to hold on tight
Sadness is inevitable
Disappointment a given
Frustration at the request of patience
Desperation when things seem final
All the while we grasp
Grasp at something to hold on to
To pull us up and out
To revive us
To make this life mean something

Alarm

I've never cared much what people think
I have always tried to be myself
I am enough
But sometimes it's hard
My image of myself wavers
I lose confidence in myself at times
I'm far from perfect
I've made mistakes, too
But each time my alarm rings
I thank God for waking me up
And I make the most of each day

Walking

A struggle
One single thought
To do better
Be better
It occupies my mind
Floods my body
It is difficult
Requires discipline
I need success
I must make it
I must do it

D.C.

One trip
One experience
Once in a lifetime
Our nation's capital
One week away from family and friends
It was unforgettable
Beautiful
Everything I thought it would be
It was just once
One time
Once in my thirty-five years

Delta

We are blinded
By technology
By shiny things
By new experiences
We all want to travel
Live past our means
YOLO they say
We want what we want
Desire and covet
Their things
Their lives
What about me, I say
When is my turn
When will I do these things?

Response

Ten years
I gave away ten years
And yet they flew
I clipped my own wings
I was afraid
I stayed
I settled
I didn't dare hope
Didn't dare walk away
This was my chance
My opportunity
Or so I thought
It never came
It wasn't my shot
My hope was dashed
But it gave way to another thought
Another vision
It's my time
Its fight or flight
And I choose both

Future

Is this the right decision?
Lately, I am filled with questions
My mind is ever searching
My heart is all knowing
What to do when they don't seem to coincide?

Can we ever know if any decision is the right one?
Which path to take
Which way to go
Which one, which one
It never stops!

I pray and I hope
For guidance
For wisdom
For strength and patience
In God I must trust

January 31st

I miss you most of all
I wonder what you would think
How you would fit in my life
If you would be proud

I fight time
I have a picture of you in my mind
I will my mind to remember you
Your face, your smile, your laugh

I will forever have questions
Questions that hurt to be asked
They might not ever be answered
I will never speak of this out loud

Date

It began with a question
A simple hello
Your inquiry requesting introduction
A smile and the sound of your voice

An agreement to get together
A quick exchange of details
Under the stars, we walked and talked
Enjoying getting to know one another

A romantic moment
"Can I kiss you?"
You surprised me
I leaned in anyway

Conundrum

Sleepless nights, endless worries
Countless questions and doubts
Thoughts about my life
And fears that aren't told

I try to stay positive
Be filled with hope
I try to choose the right path
Weigh the consequences

Is it really about wrong or right
Simply black or white?
Or are there many ways of being
Infinite possibilities?

Momma

Unconditional love
The voice of caution
Warm hearth, full bellies
Dedicated lifestyle

Our treasure, our compass
Happy childhood memories
The biggest fan and supporter
I cherish you above all else

Breathe

Counting the seconds go by
Moving forward slowly, snails pace
Am I physically moving?
Can I trust my eyes?

Motion sickness comes on rapidly
Waves and tire treads move past
Don't look too close
Inhale
But stare far off and focus
Exhale

Weight

Save me from my mind
The endless stream of consciousness
I yearn for the quiet
The beating of my heart

Beat, beat and yet be still
Muffled by my own being
Seeking weightlessness I sink
Into the endless sleep

Two thousand ten

Bad news and words that hurt
I stare at the TV and the pictures on the screen
get fuzzy
My vision gets blurry and it's pitch black
The darkness surrounds me and I feel empty

Cries of the deepest sadness rise from my chest
They escape from my lips and whimper
The heaviest of tears carrying the pain
Stifled by the blanket I bury my face in

Future

The days go by
Time moves forward
Enjoy it
Look forward to it

Make plans for your days off
Go to that concert
Buy that designer purse
Travel and see the world

Life is short
Things change from one day to the next
One year to the next
Live your life and be happy
Find fulfillment and be content

www.ingramcontent.com/pod-product-compliance
Lightning Source LLC
Chambersburg PA
CBHW051718130826
49812CB00034B/1238
* 9 7 8 9 3 9 5 9 5 0 0 1 5 *